INTERNATIONAL AND DOMESTIC WAR BRINGS SOCIAL INFLUENCE

JOHN LOK

Copyright © John Lok
All Rights Reserved.

This book has been published with all efforts taken to make the material error-free after the consent of the author. However, the author and the publisher do not assume and hereby disclaim any liability to any party for any loss, damage, or disruption caused by errors or omissions, whether such errors or omissions result from negligence, accident, or any other cause.

While every effort has been made to avoid any mistake or omission, this publication is being sold on the condition and understanding that neither the author nor the publishers or printers would be liable in any manner to any person by reason of any mistake or omission in this publication or for any action taken or omitted to be taken or advice rendered or accepted on the basis of this work. For any defect in printing or binding the publishers will be liable only to replace the defective copy by another copy of this work then available.

Contents

Preface

Introduction
This book concerns to research how war influences
any countries' economy development.
In Part one , chapter one concerns what international war influences. I shall explain whether wars can impact economy threat. I shall indicate how First World War influenced Europe economy ; what US economic consequences of war are ; how can economy policy influence peace and security ; What relationship is between civil wars and economic growth; how economic impact of the war and higher military spending is.

In part two, chapter two concerns the country's internal civil war, I shall explain what the relationship is between internal war and human welfare. I shall indicate how internal war influences human welfare ; whether internal civil wars can influence the country's long run economic development ; when and how can be stopped the civil internal war to influence economy growth. In my focus, I shall give my opinion to solve this question: Whether do wars bring either advantages or disadvantages or both to impact our economy growth ?

I write this book aim to give my opinion to let readers attempt to find answers to judge whether international war or country internal civil war will influence economy to be worse.

Prologue

CHAPTER ONE

International war economy influences

1.1 Can wars impact global economy threat?

1.1.1 How did First World War influence Europe economy ?

Can wars bring either advantages or disadvantages or both to impact our economy growth ?In history, I feel that international war can influence any country's economy development has either positive or negative impact in possible.

On the inflationary hand, for the First World War economy growth influence example, in the First World War and since most notably the German hyperinflation of the 1920 year, this type of monetary regime shows a far smaller tendency towards inflation. In the First World War period, volatility of inflation and output were higher in the short run. So, First World War had little negative impact to influence world inflation in the war period. However, in the First World War period, the supply of money was determined not by the rates of economic growth only, but by the amount of available gold and could not be adjusted in response to economic needs. So, new sources of gold would increase money supply and inflation and decrease interest rates , the opposite of what modern central banks would do to provide stable economic growth in First World War. So, it explained that the First World War occurrence caused the change from non-inflationary to inflationary long term development. Thus, it seems First World War brings more money supply and gold supply to stable economic growth in the future long term period.

On the labor productivity influence hand, leaving monetary issues aside, the First World War created the working time intellectual mood to change labor productivity, it would be a 15-18 hours working week for more enlightened leisure to Europe labors. Some prominent modern economists on the accuracy of the predictions on GDP growth per capital was remarkably accurate given to be fallen down that it was made at the time when economy growth theory did not even exist in the First World War period. Thus, it seems First World War also causes working time to be raised to the developing countries during the industrialization period. Then, the long time working time brought to the developing countries' workers to it is poor for labor health. Hence, although employers can raise productivity, but they need many workers to work long time to cause unhealthy. The majority found that the prediction on leisure is of the variations between world regions , due to income level exist, making European variety of capitalism. So, the First World War caused income inequality within countries and between nation states, trends in working hours , world poverty and ever growing needs (consumerism) and the like. Thus, the developed western countries' workers can work lesser time to compare to the developing Asia countries' workers. Consequently, First World War brought negative impact to influence the developing Asia countries' worker unhealthy and physical and mental illnesses number had been increasing as well as it brought positive impact to influence the labor productivity had been increasing to the Asia countries' employers, due to their workers need to work long time every day.

It seems on the positive impact hand, that the First World War caused the inflation occurrence to bring more money supply and gold supply to be raised to influence global economic growth. But, on the negative impact hand, it also brought low working hours in European developed countries and high working hours to the Asia developing countries which are needed to do different occupations in developing countries as well as the income inequality caused unfair social challenge had also occurred in developed countries, such as Europe, UK, US etc. and developing countries, such as China, Japan, Korea etc . Thus, First World War had brought developed countries better economy development and better salary and less working hours to labors because Europe had reached the mature stage of industrialization to avoid labors who needed to work overtime. Otherwise, it had brought developing countries poor economy development and poor salary and labors need work long time to raise productivities.

In conclusion, it implied that the First World War had bought some bad influences to developing countries' economic system, e.g. social income inequality, working hours inequality, inflation and GDP per capita going down in the past Europe economic history development, but it also bought welfares to developed countries' European labor working time intellectual mood to change labor productivity, it would be a 15-18 hours working week for more enlightened leisure to Europe labors. So, it seemed to cause negative economic influence to developing countries, but it cause positive economic influence to developed counties during the First World War time.

● Are US poor economic consequences of war?

What are the macroeconomic effects of US government spending on the war? I believe modern times are that the human cost military spending has created positive economic outcomes for the US economy. I shall indicate how the human costs of war influences positive economic outcomes for the US on these aspects which include: GDP, consumption , investment , inflation and income distribution aspects.

In fact, US heightened military spending can create employment additional economic activity and contributes to the military weapon development of new technologies, which can bring advantages into other industries in US. For long term economic influence, US military weapon research and development on creating employment would potentially have the same low cost economic benefit in US. For example, US economy had higher GDP growth in the Afghanistan and Iraq war period. Another benefit is that US had appropriate conditions for future growth after the Second World War great depression period. It was a sharp decline in income inequality and the trend in declining inequality standard after the Second World War great depression period. Thus, America's human cost military spending could bring indirect military weapon research and development on creating employment benefit and it would potentially have the same low cost economic benefit in US. However, in the war period, the higher levels of government military weapon spending with war tends to generate some positive economic benefits in the short-term period, specifically through increases in economic growth during spending booms after war period.

Why it can bring GDP growth in the US war period. In general, by the end of World Ward II, US GDP was over 120 % and tax revenue increased more than three times to over 20% of GDP. However, GDP growth there was are increase in the trend lines after the war had finished when unemployment was eliminated, recovery was well underway prior to the war, are the key counterfactual is whether similar spending on US public works would have generated even more growth. However, US macroeconomic history over the past seventy years, that there are a number of negative economic effects from conducting any wars. But, there have also positive benefits of increases US government spending on military industry. Moreover, when an economy has excess capacity and unemployment , it is possible that increasing military spending can provide an important stimulus. When military and defense spending is important in providing security for the US nation as well as helping to support and protect US's national affect.

So, in war economic view point, it will bring this question: Is efficiency or justification for any particular macroeconomic effects of war spending for US? To answer this question, I shall suppose security is not only dependent on an adequate military capability , but security can also keep on economic stability. For example, price controls strategy and rationing strategy had a significant role to play to influence consumption in US, during war period. For example, it was difficult for household to purchase products , such as washing machines, irons or water heaters because the raw resources, e.g. steel and production capabilities are needed to be used to produce military weapons instead of these products effort to prepare to fight the enemy in the Second World War. So, the raw resources, e.g. steel price will be rasied, due to shortage to supply to produce the home consumer products , Then, it will bring the home consumer products price to be raised. So, war will bring negative impact to influence home consumer product prices to be raised, due to shortage of steel resources supply when they are supplied to produce weapon to win enemy in war period. Consequently, In war period negative resource shortge hand, as the same time, the war production board was able to assign priorities to scare materials, such as rubber, steel and aluminum to ensure which went to production of the military, rather than to civilian products. In addition, wages were controlled and personal savings were encouraged through the purchase of war bonds which further limited the size of individual's disposable income during the Second World War period.

Moreover, in the war period, it also bring food price raising, due to food supply shortage and poor living standrd to poor people, even rich people. Due to people were also encouraged to conserve food and produce as much of that own food as possible because food items were generally scare. Freezes were also stayed for wages. Combined with a general reduction in consumption, it can be said living standards for whose already employed, at least in material terms did not improved , even to rich people. It means that war will influence people quality of life to be fallen down. Even, in terms of total GDP. Such as World War II (WWII) did not create a permanent increase or change in the growth the trend after the war had ended. However, the positive lasting effort for WWII was a more even distribution of wealth. This reallocation of income created the ideal conditions for the formation of an advancement consumer economy till to nowadays.

However, on war long time influence hand, the WWII influenced US economy to be changed to be better, such as material well being was affected by tax increases, new price and wage controls which constrained private sector consumption and investment is encouraged, due to World War II had destroyed the traditional material development, so it also encouraged new investors to invest to any Asia or Europea new businesses.

● Can war economy policy influence peace and security?

I believe war economics policy may contribute to international peace and security as positive impact more than negative impact. The reasons are as below:

A first positive attitude behavioral possibility , any war economic policy can increase international interdependence through trade and finance raises the potential costs of war to a degree that makes welfare an irrational option of foreign policy can raise economic growth and builds good trading relationship between countries. Moreover, the use of superior economic and military power to harm an actual or potential aggressor's economy and make it stops preparing of waging war, e.g. US restricted Mexico imported to itself country, US invented military weapons to threaten to Korea to avoid nuclear war occurrence. In the past, US spent to military expenditure which could rise to employ soldier numbers to reduce unemployment as well as assisted military weapon manufacturers needed to employ many manufacturing workers to manufacture many military weapons for US government military fighting need.

Hence, the relationship between war and economy will bring this basic question: Whether either can economics provide a growing tool for avoiding war or whether may consumption for resources and markets result in an increased likelihood of war? Following the increase of international trade and financial transfers in modern times. However, there has been a growing to concern the economic wisdom of war.

Liberal economists oppose the idea that war might be a good business and advocated the promotion of peace and advocated the promotion of peace by international economic links among the different countries. Although, history has shown that enlightened economic self-interest was not always alike to contribute to the ultimate avoidance of war. But, a short overview of the liberal peace theory indicates, it takes a look at the amount ability of economic instruments as a means to enforce peace by an economically superior country or group of countries, e.g. within the framework of the United Nations or of regional organization for security and cooperation in Europe, the African Union or the organization of American States.

1.1.4 How civil wars influence positive or negative impact?

On country itself civil war negative impact hand, what is the impact of civil wars on economic growth at domestic and in nearby countries? Some economists believe civil war can have a profound negative influence on the economic fortunes of a country or its neighbors, e.g. owing to a loss of human capital, a destruction of infrastructure and reductions in investment and trade and daily market activities. Within the period of measurement have economic consequences , the economists scale the civil war variable to be better identify their relative impacts.

They indicate the distance between countries which is a factor provides the most accurate measure of the negative economic consequences of civil wars on other countries.

On country itself civil war positive impact hand, in economic view point, the country itself civil war indicates the income and capital input terms. Since, everything is in per capita terms. Due to civil war encourage technological development. Technology changes are in the investment in labor effectiveness. The capital includes physical and human capital . How civil war influences efficiency growth . The growth in labor's enhanced efficiency is from technology change and capital depreciation. So, anything that can raise labor growth or its improved efficiency, increases the denominator or capital per capita and so reduced its growth and that of incomer per capita. Depreciation or the gradual wearing down of capita; through use or age also limits capital growth. Some economists suggest that war migration is a good growth of labor to influence the immigration country's economic growth. For example, the inflow of refugees from a nearby civil war can lead to in-migration and adversely affect income per capita growth. Migration may , however, influences the in-migration country economic growth if the migrants bring in human capital, due to civil war.

Consequently, from a theoretical perspective, civil wars can adversely affect income per capita growth at home through a number of avenues. So civil war will cause bad influence to home country, the reasons are as below:

The reasons include:

First, a civil conflict can destroy physical and human capital. Second, by the international trade flows, and day-to-day marketing activities, civil wars can inhibit growth. Third, civil wars may divert the inflow of foreign direct investment (FDI) owing to heightened perceived risks of investors. Because (FDI) perceived is an imported source of savings that finances investment. So, a fill in FDI results in reduced growth. Heightened instability and risks will also limit investment at home and cause a flight of savings abroad. Fourth, civil wars cause indirect government defense expenditures from productive social overhead capital e.g. roads, public schools and bridges, gardens to less productive defense spending. Fifth, such wars may cause the internal displacement of people as their homes either come under serious control or are destroyed. So that income per capita is adversely influenced. Sixth, civil wars often result in the breakdown of the health lead to lack of medical care, less clean drinking water and reduced sanitation , all of which have negative consequences on economic activities and growth .

Thus, any country itelf civil war can bring negative impacts more than positive impacts. Due to economic impacts may even increase further from some conflicts as nearby countries reduce trade with others in the regions and potential investors brand , even non-neighboring countries have as poor investment risks. Thus, there are four potential channels , such as human capital, physical capital, labor growth and an intercept shift are influenced by civil wars as well as which can influence income per capita growth in other nearby countries. To conclude, neighboring countries need to concern how to avoid civil war is caused to occur among themselves because civil wars will have negative impact to influence their economic growth.

● How economic positive and negative impact of the war to higher military spending?

Most models show that military spending to divert resources from productive uses, such as consumption and investment , and ultimately slows economic growth and reduces employment. So, it seems war causes disadvantages more than advantages to influence economy growth to any countries in possible.

Some economists showed global insight produced a set of projections that compared a scenario with an increase in annual military spending equal to 1.0% of GDP current about $135billions relative to its baseline scenario . This is approximately equal to the increase in defense spending that has taken place compared with the pre-Sept. 11th terrorism Iraq war baseline to US government higher military spending. However, who also indicated military spending is not generally perceived to cost jobs.

In standard economic models, war its positive impact can be thought of in the same way as spending on the environment from war bad influence. When tax and emission restrictions are often used to achieve environment protection during and after war. It is also possible to reach environmental targets by paying people to do things that will reduce pollution. For example, it is possible to reduce greenhouse gas emissions by paying people to buy more fuel efficient cars and appliances, or paying than to install insulation and other energy saving devices. So, during the war period, more greenhouse gas fuel efficient cars will increase demand in car market. Thus, war can reduce air and water pollution cost and encourage greenhouse gas fuel consumption. In the case of both increased military spending and paying people to take steps to reduce greenhouse gas emissions, resources would be reduced to supply to these countries' domestic market directed uses.

In standard economic models, war it's negative impact to this redirection of other resources, due to the original resources are used to increase military spending to manufacturing any new weapons and it will cause this original resources are shortage to prepare for these countries' manufacturing countries. So, these resources shortage challenges will cause these military spending countries' economy to operate less efficiently and therefore lead to slower growth and fewer jobs supplies. Thus, war will bring resource shortage challenges and fewer jobs supplies bad influence. In policy debates, it is important to recognize the potential jobs losses are caused from military spending factor mainly. Also the potential economic costs are often a factor in debates over environment policy.

Due to war causes the military countries' air and water pollution challenges. So, the military countries' wars occurrence will raise the water and air pollution cost of chance. It is often believed environmental pollution challenge has relationship between wars and increases in military spending. So, in this way, any country is carrying on military spending is comparable in most models to any other form of any country's spending, such as spending on public products or improving the environment pollution expenditures. Thus, it seems war will bring environment pollution economic cost more than environment protection economic benefit to any military expending countries.

CHAPTER TWO

Country itself internal civil war influences

2.1 The relationship between country itself internal civil war and human welfare

2.1.1 How internal civil war influences human welfare?

Nowadays, a growing number of economists and political scientists often ask this simple question: Why there is so much civil wars in any country itself the world? Poverty is commonly held to be a leading cause of internal wars. Indeed, it has close relationship between low per capita incomes and higher propensities for internal war's countries. Such as developing country Africa, it has many times more internal wars. So, it brings poverty and low living standards and poor health and poor air and water pollution environment to let African to live. Then, hunger and disease will also be caused easily in Africa.

However, internal civil wars also bring negative influences to developed countries, such as Australia, US Canada, UK , Japan, Korea etc. countries. The reason is because the internal civil war counties which refugee flows will choose to immigrate to those developed countries. Such as developing countries, South Korea and Africa and India , there have many times more internal civil wars .So it brings poverty and low living standards and poor health and poor environment to let African , South Korean, Indian to choose to live to these developed countries. Then, hunger and disease will be caused easily in developing and developed both countries, due to developed countries permit these developing countries' refugee who immigrate to themselves countries to live from internal civil war counties refugee immigration easily.

Moreover, internal civil war can also influence developed countries, such as Australia, US, Canada , UK refugee flows will choose to immigrate to these developed countries lawlessness as well as the illicit trades in drugs , arms and minerals will appear into these developed countries neighboring conflict zones . The destructive consequences of internal civil welfare may be a great as to potentially be a factor in the growing gap between the world's richest and poorest nations.

2.1.2 Can internal civil wars influence the country's long run economic development?

Has it relationship between long run economic growth and internal civil war? Some economists recommend that it focuses on impacts on capital and population, the basic of economic production and whether the internal civil war country is possible rapid recovery as well as the internal civil wars cause economic impacts which can also been found for human capital, including measures of education, nutrition, health and productivity to the internal civil war countries.

What are intenal civil war negative impacts? Some behavior economists had experimented one interesting research to indicate that any internal civil war country will reduce human resource productivity growth , will reduce overall GDP in possible. Their research indicated the internal war armed group leaders are most motivate citizens to be soldiers for their side. Participation becomes easier to motivate the lower is citizen's opportunity cost of fighting . So there models predict that the amount of citizens' time devoted to fighting increases as the returns to fighting rise relative to the returns to reduce human resources supply to society to assist enterprises to raise any productive activities.

Consequently, in economic view point, if the internal civil war countries citizen will be trained to be soldiers. Then, it will reduce citizen to do other occupations in the internal war period. Also, the internal civil war countries will reduce their citizen have time and effort to do other social occupations to assist countries' economy development in the internal civil war period. Moreover, the internal civil war countries citizen, such as human resource number will be shortage to supply to satisfy their countries' enterprises' needs in the internal civil war period. It will influence economic growth to be go down during the internal civil war period to the internal civil war countries for either short term or long term. Even, the natural resource supply, e.g. water, food, vehicle gas etc. will be concentrate on spending to satisfy the soldiers' needs. It will cause natural resource shortage to supply to satisfy to citizen's life needs daily in the natural civil war period. So, the internal civil war will bring disadvantage to influence economic growth to the internal civil war countries.

2.1.3 How can reduce the risks of the civil internal war to influence economy growth?

How can reduce the risks when internal civil war occurs in the country? What factors explain variations in the duration of civil internal wars, and why should policymakers care? I shall suppose to the duration of civil internal wars , which should be implicated in their destructiveness to the civil internal war country as well as long time duration of civil internal wars should have long time poor economic influence to the civil internal war country.

At any given point in a civil internal war, the civil internal war country government (A) and the civil internal war country rebels(B) each must choose between stopping or continuing to flight.

This implies four possible outcomes from their joint decisions at any time.

The first outcome is that if (B) continues flight and (A) stops, (B) wins and the government (A) is overthrown.

The second outcome is that if government (A) flights and (B) stops, (A) wins and the revolt is defeated (B) .

The third outcome is that if both (A) and (B) choose to stop flight at the same time, the civil internal war ends to be a negotiated settlement.

The fourth outcome is that if neither decides to stop, the civil internal war continues (Stam 1996 , 34-37).

Stam (1996, 353) again indicated the four outcomes can be represented as an two person game. Continued flight is the dominant strategy for both sides.

Thus, it seems negotiated settlement is the best solution to solve any civil internal war because it won't have either win or loss outcome to either of party, it will have win outcome to both countries.

In economic welfare view point, they will discuss how to earn the much economic benefits to achieve the reasonable negotiation fairly. It is a two parties win-to-win method to both supported government and not supported government parties both. Because usually the cause of any internal civil war , due to the not supported (disagreed) government party feel whose government is unfair to give reasonable and fair much economic welfare to them in society. So, they (part of citizen) only choose to cause internal civil war to let their country to know that who feel dissatisfactory at the time.

In economic view point, unfair resource allocation challenge will cause any internal civil war easily in any country. Thus, it means that any country government ought to know when and how to allocate its limited resources to let its citizen to feel fair to use (spend) in society when resources are not shortage to supply to them to consume. Also, it means how to allocate (spend) limited resource to prepare any countries' citizen to enjoy to consume. So, it is one important question to any country government to concern if which wanted to reduce internal civil war occurrence chance on nowadays societies. Thus, it seems that any country itself internal civil war will bring disadvantages more than advantages.

Bibliography

Stam , A. C. 1996, Win, Lose or Draw: Domestic politics and the crucible of war . Ann Arbor: University of Michigan Press.

www.ingramcontent.com/pod-product-compliance
Lightning Source LLC
Chambersburg PA
CBHW031641170726
47990CB00018B/1604